I0235515

IMAGES
of America

MILO, BROWNVILLE, AND LAKE VIEW

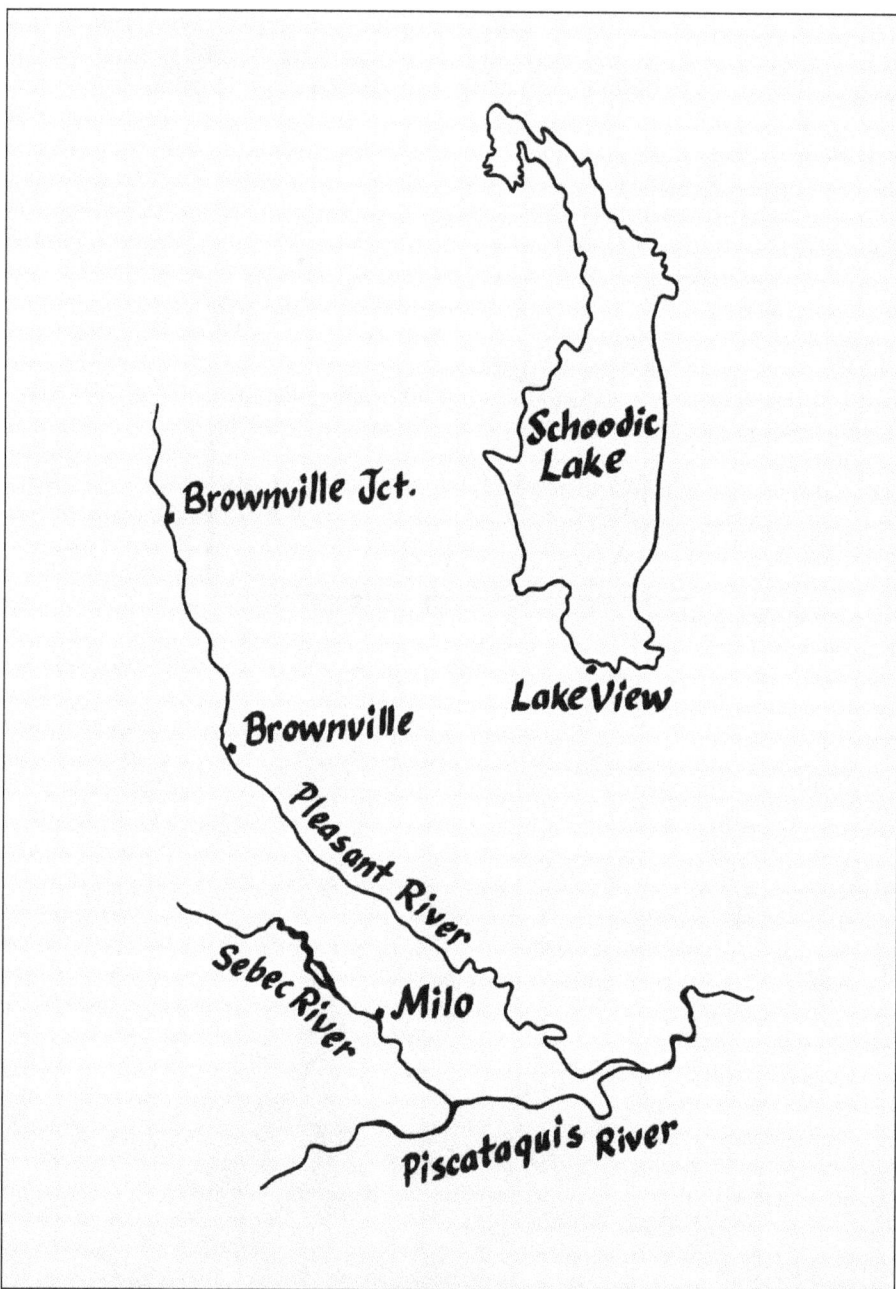

This map shows the communities of Milo, Brownville, and Lake View and their proximity to the Pleasant River, Sebec River, Piscataquis River, and Schoodic Lake.

On the cover: This view of Milo was familiar, in one form or another, to those entering Main Street from Elm Street for well over 100 years. However, the buildings were all destroyed in a fire on September 14, 2008. This picture was taken in 1919 during the welcome home celebration for World War I soldiers. Many celebrations have taken place on the Main Street of Milo, and it is certain that whatever redevelopments come, the good people of this community will continue in the spirit of "a friendly town." (Courtesy of the Milo Historical Society.)

IMAGES
of America

MILO, BROWNVILLE, AND LAKE VIEW

Milo Historical Society
and Brownville Historical Society

ARCADIA
PUBLISHING

Copyright © 2009 by Milo Historical Society and Brownville Historical Society
ISBN 978-1-5316-4222-8

Published by Arcadia Publishing
Charleston SC, Chicago IL, Portsmouth NH, San Francisco CA

Library of Congress Catalog Control Number: 2008939167

For all general information contact Arcadia Publishing at:
Telephone 843-853-2070
Fax 843-853-0044
E-mail sales@arcadiapublishing.com
For customer service and orders:
Toll-Free 1-888-313-2665

Visit us on the Internet at www.arcadiapublishing.com

*This book is dedicated to all those who have taught us to appreciate the
history of our towns, thereby teaching us more about ourselves.
Although many have filled this roll, we would especially like
to remember two of our dedicated local historians:
Dr. Ralph Monroe (Milo Historical Society founding member and
past president) and Reuben Lancaster (Brownville/Brownville Junction
Historical Society founding member and past president).*

CONTENTS

ACKNOWLEDGMENTS

The Milo and Brownville/Brownville Junction Historical Societies are eternally grateful for the diligence of many individuals who have contributed in the preservation of their communities. Because of their dedication, we have documents, photographs, and artifacts relating to the birth and growth of Milo, Brownville, and Lake View. Several individuals were especially helpful and informative when approached for assistance in identifying and providing photographs. They include Isabelle Newman Roberts, who grew up in Lake View, and Marcia Evans, a former resident. Thanks go to Susan Dean McLeod for providing photographs and information about her grandfather Lawrence McDonald and his garage business. Unless otherwise noted, all images appear courtesy of the Milo and Brownville/Brownville Junction Historical Societies. Answers to many queries were also provided through conversations with Fred Trask, Roland Larrabee, and Walter MacDougall. Information was also found at the Lake View Town Office, in books by William R. Sawtell, Lloyd Treworgy, and Rethel C. West, and in the writings of Rev. Amasa Loring and George Varney. Also without the assistance of the Milo Historical Society Museum curator Gwen Bradeen, many questions would have gone unanswered. Lastly, it should be acknowledged that this book came about from the collaborative and dedicated efforts of a committee made up of the following members of the Milo and Brownville/Brownville Junction Historical Societies: Victoria Eastman, Allen Monroe, and Kathryn Witham representing the Milo Historical Society and Grace Leeman and Carol Horne representing the Brownville/Brownville Junction Historical Society.

INTRODUCTION

In the early-morning hours of September 14, 2008, several historic buildings seen on the cover of this book were destroyed by fire. They had been features of Milo's Main Street character since the early 1900s. These were the places where people came to do business, to socialize, or, in the case of the theater, be entertained or informed.

This was the core of the community. With these landmarks gone, one might believe that all is lost. However, photographs provide an everlasting guide to history. In these records, viewers can relive times of prosperity, times of loss, and look forward to times of rebirth and growth.

Also enduring are the oral histories that pass through generations of families and communities. Stories are told, retold, and eventually written down in diaries, correspondences, or in books. This book is a glimpse at familiar faces and landscapes. It is also an introduction to the character of three communities that have so much in common yet are so distinctly different.

The ties that bind Milo, Brownville, and Lake View are water, lumber, and rails. Each of these is so linked that at one time there could not be one without the others.

Although the Snow brothers visited the area in 1799, having been encouraged by their father's description of the land and rivers, it is the Sargents who are considered Milo's first family of settlers.

Philip, Stephen, and Moses Snow did indeed settle on the banks of the Pleasant River in 1803. However, in 1802, Benjamin Sargent and his 14-year-old son, Theophilus, arrived to build a new home for their family near the Piscataquis River.

When Benjamin returned to Methuen, Massachusetts, where his wife and three other children waited, he left Theophilus behind. Thus a legend was born and the seed planted in the imagination of author Elizabeth George Speare. Her book *The Sign of the Beaver* is loosely based on Theophilus's experience alone in the wilderness.

Oral history reports that Theophilus went out one day, leaving the door open behind him. A bear, smelling food, entered the cabin, and ate all of the boy's provisions. Without his staples, Theophilus became weak with hunger. At the same time, the legend continues, a tribe of Native Americans, probably Penobscot, were in the area collecting bark for canoe making when they came upon the boy. Taking pity on him, the chief had his son Attean Oseon stay with Theophilus until his father returned from Methuen.

In fact, Benjamin had arrived in Massachusetts to discover the city under quarantine for typhus. By the time it was lifted, the Sargents, with their dog Hunter, departed much later than originally planned. They arrived at their new home and reunited with Theophilus, as the Piscataquis River began its winter freeze.

On December 28, 1804, Alice Sargent was the first child born in the settlement, in the area now known as Milo.

The first recorded Brownville settlers were the Heath family, who arrived around 1795. They lived in the northern part of the area. In 1806, Josiah Hills and Francis Brown started the settlement, later building mills and dams. The next to arrive were Dr. Wilkins and Rev. Hezekiah May, who provided services to the population, which numbered 131 in 1810. Brownville was first organized as a plantation on June 29, 1824. It was named in honor of Francis Brown, a founding father and industrialist.

As the lumber industry declined, slate quarries were established. In 1843, the Bangor and Piscataquis Slate Company opened on the eastern side of the river. This industry provided roofing slate and slate boards for schools. It was sold to Adams H. Merrill in 1876 and remained in operation for many years. The railroads came in 1887, hence the establishment of Brownville Junction, once known as Henderson. Another business was U.S. Peg and Shank Leather Company, which was sold to J. Lewis and Sons, providing employment for many years, as did the sawmill, which operated along the river.

Several miles from Brownville, lumber continued to be a key ingredient for industry. Having depleted their supply of white birch in Egypt, the Merrick Thread Company found a new source on the shores of a natural spring-fed lake near Milo and Brownville. The lake was called Schoodic and the community that grew there became Lake View Plantation.

There in 1889, the Merrick Thread Company built its spool mill, as well as tenement houses and a boardinghouse for its workers. About the same time, Canadian Pacific Railway completed tracks through Lake View. This was an important asset for mill product export.

Within a short period of time, a close-knit community grew, complete with a public hall, church, school, post office, general store, and later, a three-bed hospital. The Merrick Thread Company owned the general merchandise store. It also provided a social club with pool tables and a library for its employees.

Besides pageants and plays at Olympic Hall, this community building hosted suppers, basketball games, and concerts. The Lake View Village Band performed here and aboard one of the town's three steamers. Lake View was not without other recreational facilities. Two baseball teams played on the local diamond; tennis and basketball courts were also available.

Although the thread company's manufacturing plant was situated in the town of Lake View, its industry ventured farther along the wooded shores of Schoodic Lake where logging camps were established. Nearby timber was harvested and taken to the mill by barge through the water or by horse team across the frozen lake.

In 1898, the Merrick Thread Company merged with several other similar businesses to form the American Thread Company. In 1902, the American Thread Company opened a mill in Milo. In 1925, the mill in Lake View closed. Many employees moved to Milo to work in the mill there. The railroad continued in Lake View until the station closed in the 1940s.

Over time, Lake View's population diminished. However, with each passing summer, it becomes the bustling community it once was with the arrival of hundreds of summer residents and tourists, many of whom have strong family ties to the beginnings of Lake View Plantation on the shores of beautiful Schoodic Lake.

The historical societies of Milo and Brownville have an important and satisfying responsibility in preserving the history of their communities. Also many individuals proudly take on the role of historian, saving artifacts, photographs, and recording stories from the past. This book is simply a glimpse at familiar faces and landscapes. So much more history can be found beyond these photographs; it would take volumes to relate the stories of the people and events that brought Milo, Brownville, and Lake View into being. For readers who are just learning about these three communities, this book is an introduction to their character, their common bonds, and their individual natures.

One

MILO

Milo, known as "the town of three rivers," was established and prospered due to the industries that grew from the power of the rivers. This scene depicts a log drive, with logs being sluiced or channeled through the Trafton Falls sluice way. History records that a dozen mills and many other businesses crowded the island that divides the Sebec River below the Trafton Falls dam.

In 1823, Capt. Winborn A. Swett built Milo's first sawmill. Even today glimpses of Milo's logging history can be seen beneath the water where logs, long ago submerged, are occasionally revealed at the base of the dam that Swett built across Trafton Falls on the Sebec River.

MAIN ST. MILO ME.

AFTER

This picture provides a panoramic bird's-eye view of Milo's early business district. One can see just how many businesses were clustered on the island. Many buildings were literally hanging on the edge over the Sebec River. The Milo Hotel can be seen on the far right. It is believed that the photograph was taken from atop the Boston Excelsior Company building, noteworthy for having an arched mill-wheel opening flanking the river.

In 1879, Boston Excelsior Company purchased mill buildings near the canal in Milo. That property was used for the manufacturing of many different wood products up to that time. Eventually a new excelsior mill was erected nearer the Bangor and Aroostook Railroad station.

Milo Textile Company began operations in June 1922 in the old Excelsior mill. High-grade machine yarns were manufactured. In its heyday, the mill employed about 70 people, and the weekly payroll was nearly $1,000. The company was financed almost entirely by local people, and nearly all of its workers resided in town.

CLUB-HOUSE OF
PISCATAQUIS COUNTRY CLUB
MILO-MAINE.

For a period of over 30 years beginning in 1890, the d'Este family had property in Milo and owned and operated the Boston Excelsior Company mill. Julian d'Este was a wealthy man from Salem, Massachusetts, who built the stately home on what is now d'Este Road in Milo. At one time, the property was home to a golf course and country club. The d'Estes were instrumental in bringing electric lighting and running water to Milo. The photograph below shows the foundation being laid for one of the Boston Excelsior Company mill buildings along the canal of the Sebec River.

For many years, the American Thread Company was thought to be the most important industry in Milo. The spool factory was erected during 1901 and 1902. The machinery for this mill came from Willimantic, where the American Thread Company had been located for some time. It also owned a sawmill erected at the same time. At the sawmill, it produced spool bars and boxboards in large quantities. In its early days, the American Thread Company employed over 200 employees.

The woods camps run by the American Thread Company were located in a couple of different locations. Two were located at Five Islands on Schoodic Lake, and another was at Kineo on Moosehead Lake. In a clipping that was published around 1920 in an unidentified newspaper, Prof. C. E. Turner, an industrial hygienist from the Massachusetts Institute of Technology, wrote that the state department of health in Maine had sent him to inspect conditions in Maine's mills. The report of conditions at the American Thread Company facilities, including the living conditions of the woods camps, was exemplary and "beyond anything he could have imagined." The living conditions were very comfortable, and the food received his enthusiastic commendation. The menu on the day he inspected included smothered beef and potatoes, baked beans, brown bread, biscuits, white bread, cookies, pickles, doughnuts, applesauce, pie, tea, and coffee. The camp kitchen and dining room was run by a temperamental, albeit efficient, cook. He did not take kindly to criticism. Guests at the American Thread Company woods camps soon learned what the regular workers already knew . . . do not mess with the cook.

Between 1902 and 1975, employees of the American Thread Company rose between 4:00 a.m. and 6:00 a.m. Those who needed only an hour from bed to mill could, if they wished, wait for the two long and disturbingly audible blasts from the 6:00 a.m. whistle.

Shown here is a group of American Thread Company workers. Pictured from left to right are (first row) Wallace Gerry, Aubrey Gould, Frank Livermore, Bennie Youngblood, Willie Lord, Louis Shaw, Gus Stevens, and Irving Clark; (second row) John Ross, Walter Youngblood, Frank Ball, Norman Richards, Harry Littlefield, Ed Youngblood, Sam McKenney, Lincoln Hogan, ? Gilman, Charles Sherburn, George Morrill, unidentified, Ellen Strout, unidentified, Abbie White, William Rolfe, and George Cook.

These are two early views of downtown Milo. Above is a very early picture. Many of the later prominent buildings, such as the Masonic Block, library, and town hall, have not yet been built. Also, there is no indication of telephone or electrical poles and lines. The picture below shows that more of the well-known buildings have been established, and power lines and poles are in place, but the streets have yet to be paved.

Shown here is Sam McKinney in the boat that he built to travel to his cottage at the head of the Sebec River, an area know as the Rips. Many generations of Milo residents have retreated from the hubbub of modern life by escaping to their camps along the Sebec River and proudly claiming the title of "river rats."

In 1853, the citizens of Milo voted to build a toll bridge over the Piscataquis River, thus putting an end to the use of ferries such as this. The toll bridge was not popular, however, and was sold in 1857. The bridge became free for general use.

A toll bridge was built across the Piscataquis River in the mid-1850s. However, many articles suggest its construction was not agreed upon in town meetings from 1820 until its eventual completion in the 1850s. Connections with the outside world were accomplished by use of ferryboats crossing the river, probably in more than one location.

Planning for the Pleasant River bridge began in 1844. For many years, articles to build the bridge were "passed over" at town meetings. Even a threat by the State of Maine to impose a fine on the town if it did not build the bridge was ignored. Completion did not actually take place until 1853, when Milo's tax payers finally voted to span the widest of the town's three rivers. The bridge collapsed in either 1899 or 1900 and was replaced by the steel bridge.

Jan 23 1906

The early pioneers in Milo were not quick to bridge the three rivers. In four regular and special town meetings in 1823 and 1824, citizens did not want to bridge the Sebec River. Finally in 1825, the county offered to build the bridge for $200.

Generations of adults and children whiled away summer hours swimming in the Sebec River. This bathing beauty was planning a dip in the river from a vantage point directly behind the Milo Hotel.

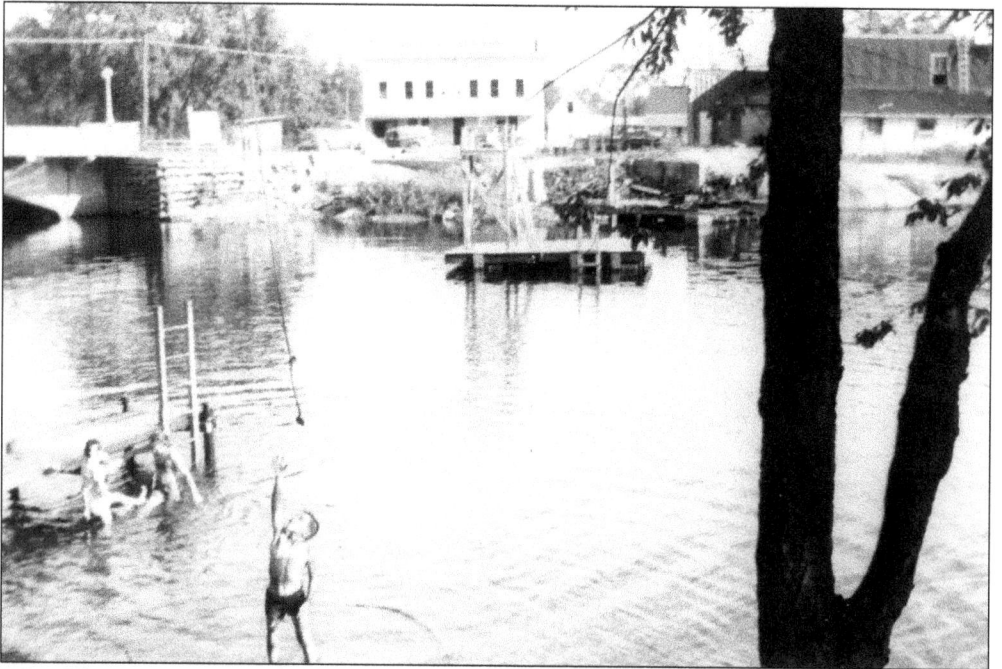

These children were cooling off at Sebec River's new swimming hole at the foot of Water Street. The float, which survived decades of use, provided many hours of playful fun to kids and adults alike on hot summer days in downtown Milo. There is a legend that tells of one unseasonably warm winter day when kids dared each other to take a dip in the open river. Another swimming hole a bit further up the tracks at the end of Clinton Street also provided a place for that neighborhood's children to swim.

When the Bangor and Aroostook Railroad decided to build its car shop in Milo Junction during the early 1900s, the little community of Derby was born. Some say that the complex of company houses, constructed to house employees and their families, was one of America's first housing developments. The development boasted a park with a bandstand, a station, a hotel, houses in a variety of sizes, and a few more-luxurious homes built for the administrators.

The Stewart Residence Milo Junct. Me.

Built in 1906, the Derby railroad shops became a model of a company looking out for its own. Homes, a hotel, and a school were built for the multitude of new workers at the shops. A beautifully manicured park, which included this festive bandstand, also was built for the entertainment of the residents of Milo Junction (which became Derby).

Here is an overview of the Bangor and Aroostook Railroad car shops in Derby. The shops included the roundhouse, a paint shop, a blacksmith shop, a smokestack, an administration building, and a myriad of tracks and railcars.

From left to right are Elwood Bamford, Lewis Harris, Hollis Clark, Millard Fogg, and Hartley McLeod. These men were all employed at the paint shop at the Bangor and Aroostook Railroad in Derby.

Freight trains visited the Derby rail yard for repair work, but passengers waited at the Milo Junction station for transportation to friends, relatives, and other communities throughout the state of Maine and beyond.

The west side of Milo's Main Street thrived with clothing, drug, furniture, hardware, and grocery stores. Individual businesses were common on both the first- and second-story levels of most of these buildings. Hairstylists, a telephone company, and a busy movie theater were among the businesses dotting lower Main Street. Through the decades of its existence, a photographer, a doctor's office, a jewelry store, a state liquor store, a pool hall, a Sears and Roebuck catalog store, a gift shop, and a florist did business in these lower Main Street buildings. More than one entrepreneur opened restaurants, including Reuben Lancaster, Val's Pizza, the House of Pizza, and Valerie Jean's American Bistro. These buildings were destroyed by an arsonist in September 2008.

The vehicles tell a story of time marching on. The composition of the highway changed, the businesses evolved, and the friendly faces of the citizenry aged, but architecture from the dawn of the 20th century remained a constant. All of these buildings, with the exception of the depicted Owen Drug Company building, were destroyed by the fire in 2008.

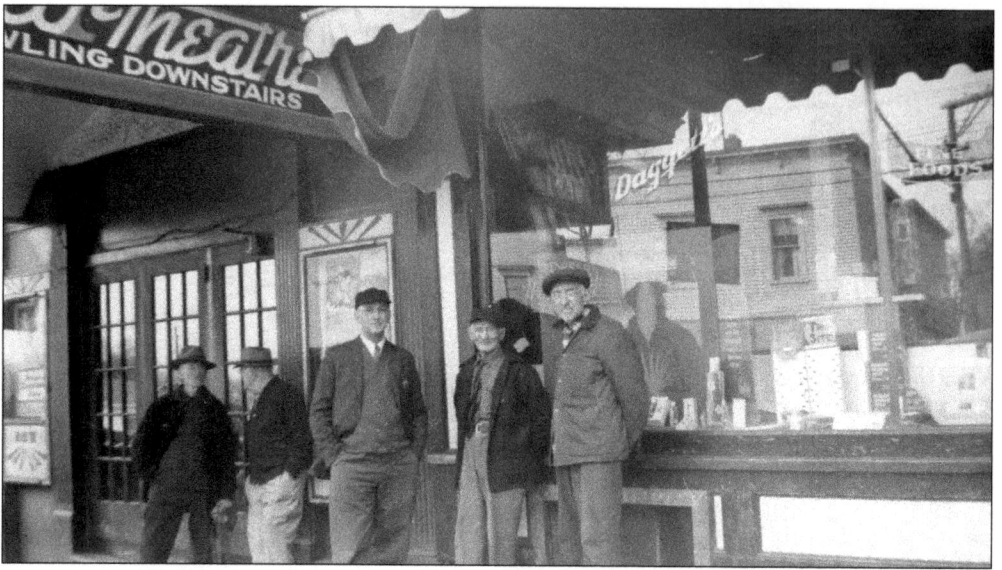

From left to right, two unidentified men, Guy Monroe, Warner Nutter Jr., and Winfield Sidney Heath are gathered in front of the Milo Theater and Daggett's Drug Store. Interestingly, the buildings on the east side of Main Street are reflected in the Daggett's window. This picture was taken on Main Street when the theater's full awning extended over the sidewalk.

These lovely young ladies formed a social club around 1905. Although not much is known about their organization, one thing is for sure: they loved posing for photographs, and they took great pleasure in throwing bridal showers for each other. Their group probably disbanded after they all married. Listed by their married names are Cora Dutch, Clara Pullen, Molly Ingalls, Arlene Nesbitt, Lavina Johnson, Georgia Daggett, Giula Leonard, Edie Richards, Jean Rosie, Mable Creighten, Abbie Gould, Anne Mills, and Sue Jenkins.

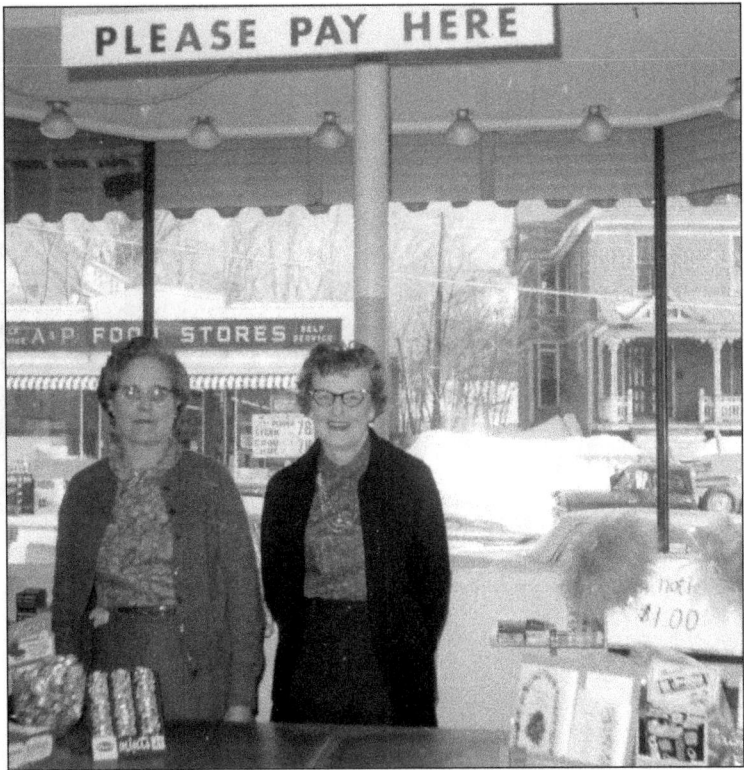

The Ben Franklin (otherwise known as the Five and Ten) sat at the head of Milo's Main Street and was owned by Forrest Treworgy. It was later run by his son Paul. Situated across the street from the A&P grocery store, Treworgy's remained a busy department store well into the 1980s. Evelyn Carey (left) and Ona Littlefield (right) worked many years for the Treworgys. When stepping through the doors of this remarkable little store, one's senses were assailed with the wonderful smell of roasted nuts.

The Milo Telephone Company started in 1902. It was owned by F. W. Hamlin and Harry W. Hamlin. From 1918 until approximately 1948, it was known as the Moosehead Telephone and Telegraph Company. Shown working the switchboards are Jane Prescott (left) and Ona Littlefield.

29

Myron Smart, on the left, and his son Forrest Smart Sr., on the right, proudly display many beaver pelts.

A SUMMER SCENE
AT DILLON HOUSE
MILO, MAINE
JANUARY 1ST, 1937.

PHOTO BY
CLEMENT

At first, one might think that these folks are enjoying a warm summer day on the front porch of Milo's Dillon House. They were enjoying warm weather, but the date was January 1, 1937. Unseasonably warm weather drew these guests out of the hotel and onto the porch to pose for this picture.

Residents of Milo have always managed to find ways to add entertainment and culture to their lives. An example is seen in this shot of the Milo Orchestra and Chorus, lead by Ethel Peterson in the 1930s.

This photograph shows how Milo celebrated the homecoming for World War I soldiers. At this time, cars were probably quite scarce, and an automobile parade was quite an attraction.

The "Chic" Theatre, Milo, Me.   Pub. by C. O. Purdy

Crowds of people flocked to the new Chic Theater, built in 1913, which entertained town folks for generations with silent movies and talkies. In later years, the Chic Theater was renamed the Milo Theater and was owned and operated by Anne Mills. It closed in 1955 when it became a victim of the public's new infatuation with television. The basement of the Milo Theater was home to a small billiard hall and bowling alley. This building was destroyed by the fire of September 14, 2008.

2.33 Class Milo, Me. July 23.

Town records indicate that the Milo Trotting Park and Fairgrounds was constructed in 1889 on the George Gubtil farm, located on Park Street. It was later known as the Kroemer farm. The facility was there until about 1920, but there were no horse races after 1913. It then became a recreational area, and baseball was played there. A report in the *Piscataquis Observer* by Leon G. C. Brown, dated June 29, 1905, stated that at a meeting held in the Milo Town Office it was voted to hold a cattle show and fair at the Milo Driving Park. It also said that "the hall beneath the grand stand will be remodeled and an excellent chance will be provided for the ladies to exhibit fancy articles."

SCORE ⁑ CARD

— FOR —

TUESDAY, JUNE 23d, 1896,

OVER THE

MILO DRIVING PARK.

				1	2	3	4	5	TIME.
2.33 Class. Trot and Pace.									
Purse, $100									
Judge Goodlow,	E. B. Ireland, Exeter,	Red and Green							
Harvard, ch g	I. Briggs, Parkman,	Black and White							
Whalebone Chief, b s	A. E. Perkins, Great Works,	Red and Gray							
Gipsy B., g m	C. Brinan, Bangor,	Black							
Harry C., br g	F. A. Dillingham, Orrington,	Red							
Denver, blk g	C. G. Andrews, Bangor	Blue							
3 Minute Class. Trot and Pace.									
Purse, $100									
Violin, b g	H. S. Brockway, Dover,	White							
Flora Bell,	W. D. McGregor, Ea. Corinth,	Black							
Riley C., ch g	H. M. Steadman, Foxcroft,	Red							
Donald Wilkes, b g	C. G. Andrews, Bangor,	Blue							
Little Eva, b m	C. G. Andrews, Bangor,	Blue							
Ellen M., b m	E. C. West, Monroe,	Old Gold and Black							
Lady Dawn, g m	H. E. Haley, Monroe,	Red and Brown							

MANAGERS:

F. W. Hamlin,	A. F. Spearing,	F. M. Strout,	B. W. Doble, Jr.

Races called at 2 P. M. Sharp.

THE STANDARD PRINTING CO., FOXCROFT, ME.

Uncertainty remains as to the origins of the name of this early Milo hotel. With imaginations working overtime, one might stir up exotic images of Asian maidens tending to the needs of tired travelers or perhaps a Chinese laundry servicing the community. The hotel was located on the island, an industrial hub located in the middle of the Sebec River. Renamed the Milo Hotel, this building burned around 1913 and became the site of the Milo Farmer's Union store. The building was purchased by Claude Trask in 1967 and renovated to house the Trask's Insurance Company office along with a variety of other businesses and apartments.

The year was 1913 and Walter and Laura Dillon, who ran the Milo House on the island, were returning from a trip to Bangor and were preparing supper when one of the boarders reported a fire in the building. The house was gutted, and the Dillons were forced to abandon the building. The Dillons decided to go into business on their own and purchased the Charles Blood home, a two-and-a-half-story house on the hill overlooking the Milo business district. Walter died in 1954, and Laura kept the hotel open but no longer served meals, except breakfast. There were 20 rooms, and at times, they were filled to capacity. In 1972, Laura Dillon celebrated 58 years in the hotel business. The Dillon House was still mentioned in the *Maine Register* in 1977 but not in 1979. The structure was torn down in 1985.

Another hotel that accommodated visitors to Milo was the establishment run by the American Thread Company. Built primarily to lodge traveling businessmen, the hotel was conveniently located near the railroad station and next to the Sebec River. In later years, the building was lowered to one story and housed the Milo Sports Shop, run by the Picard family. Other businesses that have occupied the building include a furniture and appliance store and a manufacturing facility.

Derby (otherwise known as Milo Junction) also featured a lovely hotel that was built by the Bangor and Aroostook Railroad to accommodate the railroad business traveler. The efficient waitresses, pictured here in the dining room, served weary travelers who could take a stroll in the nearby park and return to their rooms to rest before heading off on the train at dawn. This building was later reduced considerably to a one-story building, being used as a community hall for many years and hosting many wedding receptions.

These young men were hired to shovel Prospect Street in Milo after a particularly huge snowfall one winter day in the 1930s. In those days, a number of methods were enlisted in order to keep the streets clear.

From atop the Milo Town Hall, photographer Dale Jenkins took this interesting picture using time-lapse photography. The photograph was taken in the very early 1940s of downtown Milo. Notice the Christmas lights strung across the Main Street. Joe Knowles's garage is aglow on the far right side of the picture. The multitude of cars parked diagonally on both sides the street is a good indicator of the hectic pace Christmas shoppers keep, no matter what decade they live in.

For many years, Virgil Larouche owned and operated a carpet store out of his Pleasant Street showroom. This cleverly designed float was probably in one of Milo's bigger parades. The town's sesquicentennial parade was in the early 1970s, and the nation's bicentennial was a couple of years later in 1976. This float could have been in either or both of those parades.

Lawrence "Mac" McDonald was a prominent businessman, inventor, and friend to many. He owned and operated McDonald's Garage on land that he bought from Carrie Peakes in 1924. Jake Waterhouse and Herbert Ellingson were hired as mechanics. He bought the wrecker pictured in front of the garage in the 1930s and used it for 40 years. It is now on display at Coles Transportation Museum in Bangor. McDonald sold the building on lower Elm Street in 1965 and moved down the street to a smaller garage.

This is another view of Milo's Main Street in its heyday. At this time, one could find just about anything from the Main Street merchants, including clothing for the entire family, groceries, furniture, jewelry, and a delicious treat from the ice-cream parlor after taking in a movie at the theater.

Ida McKinney ran a small sundry shop for a number of years on Park Street in Milo. She was a single woman and enjoyed supplying her customers with fashionable and pretty merchandise. Her patrons were able to buy a box of bonbons, a nice lace hanky, or a stylish new hat. It appears from the picture that patrons could even entertain themselves with a lively musical piece on the piano.

James Loren Martin was born on July 8, 1851, in Bradford. His Milo home, long ago replaced with a supermarket, was on the corner of High Street and Main Street. Martin was an undertaker and coroner, and on the first floor of his home there was a funeral parlor, a barbershop with two chairs, a casket-making shop, and a harness-making area. He died on April 22, 1939, in Milo.

The Wentworth House was built in 1917 or 1919 by Caleb Wentworth, who had a feed store on the island. The house was a magnificent piece of architecture, with pillared archways between living rooms, cherry woodwork, and tin ceilings. The kitchen boasted products from Monson Slate. The home was torn down in 1998 to make room for a pharmacy chain store.

In December 1926, Milo honored eight couples who had been married 50 or more years. Walter Dillon, proprietor of the Dillon House, honored them with a turkey dinner (below), and movie cameras recorded the event. In 1927, the eight couples were honored again, and after a celebration in Milo, they left Milo, escorted by a motorcycle squad of state policemen, to go to Augusta. They were guests of Gov. Ralph Owen Brewster at a luncheon and then continued their trip to Portland. They were guests of Harry Bridges, manager of the Falmouth Hotel, where they rested overnight for the next leg of their journey to Boston. In 1928, Dillon again gave his annual party honoring couples married 50 years or more, and for the first time, newlyweds were honored too.

Fraternal organizations have played an integral part in Milo's history. On May 4, 1906, the Masons voted to sell the part of the Chase Hall owned by the lodge for $2,000 and purchase part of the Bank Block for $4,000. The hall was dedicated on February 22, 1912. The Masons sold their building on Main Street in 2008 and bought the former Full Gospel Assembly Church on outer Park Street.

This picture is of the Odd Fellows hall on the corner of Main and Elm Streets. The Odd Fellows acquired the lot on the corner of Main and Elm Streets in 1888 for $1,000. The building housed the Odd Fellows, Rebeccas, United States Postal Service, Bangor Hydro Electric Company, and Crotona Club. In 1968, the building was torn down to make room for a bank.

Band Stand and Chase's Hall, Milo, Maine.

Chase Hall was originally built as a meetinghouse for the citizens in the 1850s. The building was bought by the Milo School District in 1917 and was used as a school until 1955, when the students were moved to the new Milo Elementary School building. During World War II, volunteers climbed to the bell tower in Chase Hall with binoculars in hand, doing their civic duty by trying to spot enemy planes that might be flying over the town. The building later belonged to the H. A. Bailey Lumber Company and was torn down and replaced with a more modern lumber shed.

Milo's first high school was built in 1893. Students attended this school until a larger and more modern high school could be built in 1906. An addition was built in 1922 to accommodate the ever-increasing number of students. At that time, Milo had the best-equipped high school in Piscataquis County. For many years, the original high school served as a middle-level facility for seventh and eighth graders. In 1968, the new Penquis Valley High School was built. Basketville, a basket-making manufacturer, moved to Milo and took up residence in the former high school building. When Basketville eventually moved to the former American Thread Company building on West Main Street, the former schools were purchased by a developer who turned them into much-needed apartment housing. They remain as apartment buildings today.

School spirit was lead by Milo's cheerleaders. This trio of cheerleaders is pictured in 1931. From left to right are Irene Kiernon, Claude Trask, and Arlene Crocker.

These young ladies were Milo Grammar School cheerleaders in 1947. From left to right are Clara Stanchfield Chase, Jean Stevens Perkins Amero, Shirleen Harris Ladd, and Janice Houston Mountain.

Sports have always played a major role in the local schools' extracurricular activities. At one time, Milo High School enjoyed an active football team. This picture from 1925 shows team members. From left to right are (first row) Lauren Tuck, Robert Haskell, Abner Ford, Keith Wingler, Lawrence McLeod, Harry Bowden, and Allen Call; (second row) Winslow Weston, Edward Prescott, Leo Heal, Donald McLeod, Arthur Owen, and Henry (Hank) Small (coach).

This picture is of the 1949–1950 baseball team. From left to right are (first row) George Milner, R. Maxim, Al Hackett, Eben DeWitt, Roger Clapp, Irving Fletcher, and James Ladd; (second row) Mr. Wescott (coach), R. Nutter, Kenneth Kealiher, Phil Paul, Herbert "Rusty" Lyford, H. Hughes, M. Hamlin, and R. Nelson (manager).

Here are two of Milo's primary schools, although technically one was in Derby (Milo Junction). The picture above shows the Milo Primary School. The building was later acquired by the Bailey Lumber Company and converted into its store headquarters. The Derby Primary School served that community for many years, and former students have many fond memories. The school was eventually torn down.

A building that housed Milo's first fire department was located on the corner of Main Street and Water Street. The fire department is now housed in the basement of the Milo Town Hall. Many years have passed, and many pieces of equipment have come and gone since those early days when Milo Fire Department's biggest piece of equipment was the *Tiger* pump. Although having pride in equipment and looking good in a uniform are not necessarily prerequisites for being a firefighter, both seem to prevail through the generations in Milo.

On March 17, 1912, the newly built Methodist church was dedicated. Over the years, its affiliation has remained with the Methodists, although now it is called the Park Street United Methodist Church. At around the same time that the church was being built, the Milo Board of Trade was electing its first slate of officers. The first order of business for the new board of trade was to raise the money to install a town clock in the bell tower of the new church. A campaign was waged by the board of trade to solicit pledges from townspeople, and in record time, $400 was raised.

The first public library was established in 1902 in the home of Mary Hobbs. Later the library was moved to the Odd Fellows Block where Elsie Sherburn was librarian. Outgrowing those quarters and being burned out from another location, the library occupied the upstairs hall of the Perrigo building. The present Milo Free Public Library opened in 1923 and is a Carnegie library building.

Milo's town hall was built in 1923. The building houses the fire department and town offices, as well as a kitchen and dining room on the first floor and a large auditorium and stage on the second floor. A large balcony occupies the third floor. Rare would be the resident, past or present, who did not have at least one memory of a function within the walls of the Milo Town Hall.

This photograph was likely taken at the dawn of the 20th century. It shows a group of Civil War veterans from the 20th Maine Regiment, Company B, in front of the Grand Army Hall at the top of Main Street in Milo. The original Company B was mustered into the 20th Regiment, Maine Volunteer Infantry, in August 1862 in time to march to Antietam with the Fifth Corps, Army of the Potomac. Company B, commanded by Col. Walter G. Morrill, was recruited among the farmers of Dover, Milo, and Sebec in Piscataquis County. At Gettysburg, Company B was sent out as skirmishers by Col. Joshua Chamberlain to protect the regiment's exposed left flank. Posted behind a stone wall, the company was too far away to participate in the initial fight but was instrumental in routing the fleeing Confederates, its sudden appearance adding to their confusion. Company B was with the 20th in all its battles, from the Wilderness to Petersburg to Appomattox. Morrill became the regiment's last commander in March 1865.

Park St. Milo, Me.

Here are two views of a prominent intersection of downtown Milo: the crossroads of Main Street, Park Street, and Pleasant Street. The above picture shows some sort of gathering, perhaps following a parade or celebration. It was obviously taken at an early time due to the horses and carriages and lack of any automobiles of any kind. Telephone and electrical poles are evident, and the hanging light over the intersection is worthy of note. The picture below, taken at the same intersection from a different angle, shows a couple exchanging neighborly greetings. The house in the center background was the home of Dr. Louis Ford. It was razed to make room for the Milo Free Public Library and the Milo Town Hall.

"Victory Day"
Nov. 11, 1918.
Milo-Maine.

Milo loves a parade and has hosted many over the years. Whether it is a simple, dignified Memorial Day parade or the full-blown celebration of a significant town anniversary, Milo residents enjoy having the chance to gather and commemorate an event. These pictures were taken in 1919 during the Victory Day parade commemorating the end of World War I and the soldiers' return home. Parade participants are seen carrying an enormous American flag down the West Main Street hill. The buildings in the background are sheds that were part of the American Thread Company spool mill. The picture below shows a group gathered with the flag after the parade and ceremony in front of the Odd Fellows hall on Main Street.

Constructed in 1853 and remodeled about 1890, the former Free Will Baptist Church is the oldest religious building in Milo. William Owen, who partially recovered his expenses through the sale of pews, privately built the modest wood-frame church. The Free Will Baptists and the Baptist Society held their services alternately in this building until 1888. At that time, the church on Pleasant Street, pictured below, was completed. The Free Will Baptist Church used the premises on High Street until it merged with the Baptist Society in 1913, forming the United Baptist Church. The building was sold to the Christian Science Organization, which later sold it to the Episcopal church. In 1996, the Milo Historical Society purchased the building for its museum, a fitting setting to house the heritage of Milo's community.

In 1923, the citizens of Milo celebrated the centennial anniversary of the settlement of the town. An elaborate pageant was held, with a reenactment of the story of the first family of settlers, the Sargents. This photograph is of Keith Wingler, who portrayed Theophilus Sargent in the play. The dog in the photograph is unidentified, but Sargent had a dog named Hunter. In a program written for the pageant, Rethel C. West wrote the following regarding the origins of the town's name: "The naming of the town was a very important event, for it seemed that the settlers were unable to agree. Some desired to name the town for Joseph Lee, who owned a large part of the township; others desired to name it for Mr. Wells, who also owned considerable land here at that time; still others had different ideas. Finally the honor of naming the town was given to Theophilus Sargent. Mr. Sargent, having perhaps read the story of the noble Roman knight, Milo, or of the beautiful Venus de Milo, named the town for one of these, which we cannot say, but can all imagine."

Two

BROWNVILLE AND BROWNVILLE JUNCTION

In 1887, the Canadian Pacific Railway started operation in Brownville. The first train went through town on June 3, 1889. Joseph Crandall brought the train in and engineer James McCluskey, pilot C. H. Small, and engineer James Burke took it east.

These photographs show a service flag dedication and honor roll in 1943 in remembrance of all soldiers in town who served or died.

Members of the class of 1940 from left to right are (first row) unidentified, Gerald Ladd, and Shirley Archer; (second row) unidentified, Glenise Nichols, unidentified, unidentified, Edith Thomas, and Violet Smith.

Members of the 1939–1940 Brownville Junction Grammar School basketball team include ? Faraday, Dawn Washburn, Ardette Small, Joyce Crandall, Kathleen Gerrish, Madeline Carey, Madelyn Knowles, Lucy Martin, and Arlene Wright.

The Farm   Katahdin Iron Works, Maine

Here is the farm at Katahdin Iron Works.

This photograph shows slate miners at Merrill Quarry in Brownville. The remnants of the mines can still be found today.

Echoes of the past are found in this photograph of Main Street in Brownville Junction in the early 1930s.

Still active today, here is a historic picture of the Canadian Pacific Railway yard in Brownville.

A group of young ladies is gathered here. Included here are Greta Connors, Georgia Rollins, Jeanette Artus, Hester Page, Francis Miller, Alma Crocker, and Mildred Strout. Take a look at the car they arrived in.

Berl Green is seen driving oxen near Silver Lake Hotel at Katahdin Iron Works.

This view from around 1900 shows the distinct features of the Katahdin Iron Works and some of its associated buildings.

Canadian Pacific Railway's houses in Brownville Junction were built by the railroad for its workers.

The Catholic church and rectory in Brownville Junction were built in 1892. They were destroyed by fire and rebuilt in 1914. Rev. John L. Doherty was the first resident priest.

The buildings pictured, from left to right, are the Briggs house, the pool hall, and Allie Price's house. They are located at the present spot of Joe's saw shop.

The Brownville Band played for many functions in town.

The Briggs Block and "Elm House" were both located at the corner of present-day Pleasant Street.

Looking up the Church Street hill in Brownville, two churches are seen in this photograph: the Methodist church and the Brownville Community Church. The Methodist church is now the home of the Brownville Historical Society Museum.

The original match factory was later incorporated into the Lewis Mill.

Looking toward Windy Hill, Union Square is visible. This area was destroyed by fire in 1915.

The covered bridge over the Piscataquis River was also destroyed in the 1915 fire.

A Lombard Steam Hauler is being used at Katahdin Iron Works to transport equipment used for lumbering.

This view looks toward Brownville Junction. The first building on the right is Hayes Store, now the business location of Simple Sacks. Across the intersection is the John Chase house, which has since been destroyed.

Looking up the river toward Brownville Junction, this view shows the mills, dam, and buildings destroyed in the 1915 fire.

Legend states that Mr. Lewis was starting the boiler and sawdust caught on fire. The fire ran wild and unstoppable, destroying the entire town in the fire of 1915.

William Sparrow built the Slate House for his family. Its uniqueness lies in the fact that is was almost entirely covered with slate. The house has had many owners over the years and still stands, albeit with a few modern features.

In 2000, John Leeman tore down the Grange hall, which is seen in this 1960 photograph.

The YMCA building was constructed in Brownville Junction between 1917 and 1918 by the railroad for the use of its workers and their families.

This is an early picture of the Brownville Grange Hall, depicting a time when it was a well-maintained structure.

The Masonic Block was one of the many buildings destroyed in the fire of 1915.

The modern-day bridge over the Pleasant River has a slight curve.

It must have been a historic occasion when the first train crossed over the new trestle bridge in 1893.

Early houses on the present-day road to Brownville Junction and the wooden dam with a train in the background can be seen in this photograph.

One of Brownville Junction's historic landmarks is the Canadian Pacific Railway yard.

Herrick Hotel and Stables was later the location of a restaurant and a garage owned by Richard Grant.

The town office and post office in Brownville were also lost in the fire of 1915.

The parsonage, shown in this 1910 photograph with the Methodist church, was torn down in the 1970s.

Schoolchildren attended the Brownville School with the annex, shown here around 1920.

A glimpse of the past can be seen in this photograph, which looks down Pleasant Street in Brownville.

The J. H. Welch Store was located in the town square.

The C. E. Herrick Company with its gas pumps is seen here near the Herrick Hotel, which is located on left. Note the old car.

This is a view of the C. E. Herrick Company parts department in Herrick's Ford garage. The picture was taken in the 1920s.

The Brownville School burned in 1932.

This is a view of the Canadian Pacific Railway's company houses.

Here is a parade along the hill on Church Street in Brownville.

Gov. William Cobb visited the Katahdin Iron Works.

Here is another scene of the Katahdin Iron Works.

Childhoods of the past are remembered in this photograph of the Henderson School.

SILVER LAKE HOTEL, K.I. WORKS ME.

This photograph reminds residents, past and present, of the Silver Lake Hotel at Katahdin Iron Works.

Here is the Canadian Pacific Railway station in Brownville Junction, where today one can linger and watch the trains go by.

Snow was the order of the day in this view of High Street, looking toward Williamsburg at the four corners.

The high school building at Brownville Junction was built in 1891. All grades were taught in the same building. The school burned down 20 years later and was immediately replaced with the building pictured above.

Georgia Rollins is shown in a photograph taken in 1935 at the Katahdin Iron Works station when the last train came through.

The game being played was between the Canadian Pacific Railway Beavers and the Bangor League on August 30, 1913, on the baseball grounds at Brownville Junction.

This is a view of the dam and mills of Brownville before the fire of 1915. The Briggs Block is also seen in this picture.

The Henderson baseball team was known as the CPRs. They had red uniforms and their knickers were padded. The team members, from left to right, are (first row) Eddie Estes (third base) and Edwin Peters (umpire); (second row) Frank Cousins (manager), Porter Dale (catcher), L. B. Chase (outfield), E. D. Humphrey (outfield), Dick Hughes (pitcher), Owen Jones (outfield), Israel Hughes (second base), Fred Crandall (first base), Granville McMillan (shortstop). The building seen in the rear between Cousins and Dale is the Winn Hobbs house. The house in back of Crandall and McMillan is the William Duff house.

This is a view of the park in Brownville Junction in 1937.

The Bangor and Aroostook Railroad station is shown at Henderson, which is now known as Brownville Junction.

This is a 1900 scene of Main Street in Henderson (now Brownville Junction). The picture includes a view of the Pleasant River House, Dillon Hall, and the theater. The Canadian Pacific Railway station is on the right.

This photograph shows the Chairback Mountain Camps at Katahdin Iron Works about 1907.

The first school in Brownville was built 1821.

Because of the proximity to New Brunswick, it was not unusual to see groups of Canadian soldiers, such as these from the 22nd Battalion at Brownville Junction on April 27, 1917. In the background one can see the railroad station and soldiers in formation on Main Street.

Here is a striking view of the railroad trestle and dam at Pleasant River in Brownville in 1980.

Frank Hughes owned one of the many camps on beautiful Schoodic Lake in Brownville.

This jitney, shown in 1922 at Katahdin Iron Works, was used to travel the train lines in the area.

The Main Street of Henderson is seen in 1902. Today the town is known as Brownville Junction.

The Shank Mill can be seen in this photograph with the north and south mills in the background. Across the river at the four corners is the Masonic building. Viewed from left to right are the drugstore, the Minnie Chase residence, the telephone exchange, Peter O. Berg's Pool Hall and Soda Fountain (with a jail in the basement), and Earl Gerrish's General Store. The second story of the Masonic hall had rooms, a library, and doctor's office.

Rivers in the area offered many recreational and photographic opportunities. Here is a view of the Pleasant River bridge over Pleasant River in Brownville Junction.

School Street is located in Brownville Junction.

Central Square in Brownville is shown here in 1926.

The underpass in Brownville Junction is shown in this photograph.

This is a view of the village of Brownville as seen from Windy Hill looking toward the four corners intersection about 1902.

Crocker Quarry, located on Church Street in Brownville, began operation in 1843 and was first owned by Phineas Morrill then transferred to Samuel Crocker, Isaac Pitman, Joseph Simms, and William Hughes. Crocker sold the entire business to the Bangor and Piscataquis Slate Company, which operated it for many years.

The North Brownville Baseball Nine members include Frank Tompkins, Ernest Billings, Handford Graves, Myron Tufts, Gil Tompkins, Johnny Stevens, and Tonnie Roberts.

Shown here in 1933 is the North Brownville School, which was the last district school. Among those seen here are (first row) Clyde Kelley, Mildred Quirion, Charles Briggs, Rex Kelley, Donald Lundin, Edith Stevens, Annette Quirion, and Grace McGlinchy; (second row) Charles Chase, Louise Briggs, Pricilla Arbo, Edward Arbo, Eda Stevens, Josephene Stubbs (teacher), Florence Kelley, Marie Kelley, Lorenzo Quirion, and Gerald Applebee.

At one time, Brownville Junction had its own high school.

Brownville Junction had a championship basketball team in 1936 and 1937. All individuals in this photograph are unidentified.

The Brownville Junction honor roll, listing those who served in World War II, was located near the center of the town. The monument was made of wood and is now gone.

This photograph shows George Herrick's residence on the main road leading to Milo. He was the owner of the Herrick Hotel.

This is a photograph of Main Street in Brownville looking south.

Brownville School had an annex.

This photograph, taken in about 1980, is looking north at the new cement bridge from the north side near Milton Smith's restaurant.

This photograph shows Bridge Street in Brownville, looking up the hill toward Williamsburg.

The Rolfe family owned one of the oldest houses in Brownville at the time of this photograph. Mr. and Mrs. Elmer Ames are in the background on the porch, along with Mr. and Mrs. Merry, seen third and fourth from the left against the fence. This house is located opposite the Brownville Cemetery. It was owned for many years by the Perkins family.

Meet a class of Brownville students, in approximately 1922 or 1923. From left to right are (first row) Marion Howard, Walter Buckley, Anna Gerrish, Medora Henderson, Alfred Nelson, Jane Stone, Myretle Stone, Dot Melanson, Vaughn MacKinnon, Helena Zwicker, Alan Ryder, Edward Ellis, Henry Willet, Everett Gerrish, and Francis Jones; (second row) Gerald Rollins, Alice Zwicker, Earl Buckley, Donovan Pierce, Duane Chase, Vernon Nelson, Fred Gould, Frances Stone, Elmer Melanson, David Stone, Nelson Brewer, Vaughn Lancaster, Chester McKeen, and Clifford Andrew; (third row) Alfred Lundin, Jimmy Comeau, Willie Smith, Irene Freeman, Goldie Chick, Marion Harvey, George Foulkes, Georgia Rollins, Evelyn Carter, Viola Carter, Edie Cyr, Frank Carter, Connie Roberts, Alice Foulkes, Helen Page, and Grace Buswell.

Col. Walter G. Morrill, born in Williamsburg, was captain of the Brownville Rifles, organized in Brownville under his leadership. Morrill left Brownville for Portland on July 15, 1861. He went on to fight with Col. Joshua Chamberlain at the battle of Little Round Top and fought in many other engagements. He was wounded at least three times. Following his retirement, he got into horse racing and lived and died in Pittsfield. Morrill was a great hero, and much has been written about him.

Welcome to Main Street in Henderson (now known as Brownville Junction).

This photograph shows a spot near School Street in Brownville Junction.

Meet the Canadian Pacific Railway office crew in the 1950s. From left to right are (first row) Tyler Harris (road master), James Early (chief clerk), Laurence Harris, Ralph Evans, Ernest Jelly (division engineer), Fred Cole, Stan Paynter, and Daniel Bagley; (second row) Elizabeth Walls, Laura Densmore, Doris Harris, Eleanor Abbott, Bernice Moran, Annie MacLean Graves, Forrest Bailey (superintendent), Lucy Larson, Iona Roberts, Carrie Ross, and Cran Baker.

Seen here is the railroad station in Brownville Junction.

These views show above and below the Onawa trestle on the Canadian Pacific Railway line with Borestone Mountain in the background.

The railroad comes to town in this photograph showing the laying of the Canadian Pacific Railway line.

Three

LAKE VIEW

Schoodic Lake, surrounded by white birch, brought the Merrick Thread Company to its shores. There the community of Lake View was born.

The hearth and surrounding decor may be too refined to be one of the Merrick Thread Company's lumber camps. Many years after this photograph was taken, Elizabeth George Speare stayed with her husband at a camp on Schoodic Lake. One rainy day, she decided to visit the library in Milo. There, she discovered the story of Theophilus Sargent. From this little seed of local lore grew her book *The Sign of the Beaver.* (Courtesy of Marcia Evans.)

The Merrick Thread Company had lumber camps deep in the woods around Schoodic Lake. Here timber was cut then transported by lake steamer or barge to the mill. In the winter, horse teams hauled wood across the frozen water. This could be treacherous for horse and man because, on occasion, the ice could not hold the weight.

Hunting and fishing on Schoodic Lake were said to be a sportsman's paradise. It is likely that fish and game provided many meals for those working in the mill's lumber camps. (Courtesy of Marcia Evans.)

In newspaper advertisements, Frank O. Garson provided not only a full description and detail of the wood-working plant but also a panoramic view of the American Thread Company mill and a written description of all of it and the community of Lake View. Among the facility's features were a boiler house, a power plant, a sawmill and main mill, a carpenter and blacksmith shop, a mill supply store, a log hauler barn, an icehouse, a boathouse and boats, stock sheds, a machine shop, sled and wagon storage, a stable, and fire protection. (Courtesy of Marcia Evans.)

This is an aerial photograph of the American Thread Company around 1920. Frank O. Garson, the sales agent of the mill, wrote in his advertisement, "A big sacrifice for quick sale. Manufacturing plant and equipment, Lake View, Maine; in the heart of timber country, 40 miles from Bangor, 175 miles from Portland. A beauty spot of America."

Across the railroad tracks, the American Thread Company's dry sheds housed the wood to dry before manufacturing spools. They were arranged in such a way to be heated by either live or exhaust steam.

This photograph is identified as the American Thread Company office force.

Beyond the mill smokestack is a piece of land known as Squaw Point. At one time, houses on the point were relocated up to the back street in Lake View. Rather than dismantle the buildings, horse teams moved them in whole to their new location.

Here is another view of Squaw Point after the buildings were moved. (Courtesy of Marcia Evans.)

This is the railroad station at Lake View and the water tower. Behind is the Lake View House, built as a boardinghouse for mill workers. The mill also had an industrial track system with steel-frame industrial cars and Plymouth gasoline locomotives that connected the mills, dry kilns, stock sheds, and skid ways for air-drying stock.

This is the childhood home of Isabelle Newman Roberts. Her father, Pat Newman, worked in the Bangor and Aroostook Railroad section of Lake View, which was located at one end of the village. His brother Ernest Newman worked with the Canadian Pacific Railway, which went right through the village. Isabelle's grandfather Vincent Newman also worked for the Canadian Pacific Railway.

Railroad employees lived in tenements known as section houses. They were similar to today's duplexes, with one family on each side. Summer brought more rail workers who could rent houses in the village. The two similar, block-shaped white houses in the background are the section houses.

This home is referred to as the Riggs house. The Riggs family owned the place after the chief executive officer of the American Thread Company lived there. This is one of many photographs of Lake View featured in newspaper advertisement for the American Thread Company mill sale.

In this structure, which housed Lake View's general merchandise store and post office, one could also find a doctor's office and hospital. The hospital was equipped with three beds, a dispensary, and a complete outfit for handling accidents and other emergency cases. The two doctors who served the Lake View community were Dr. Harvey C. Bundy and Dr. Albert Card. Both men eventually moved to Milo.

Mail and passengers were brought by horse and carriage to the Lake View post office and general store building.

The general store, post office, doctor's office, hospital, and social club were all housed in one building, to the left of the water tower. On the right is the boardinghouse. According to information on the back of this postcard, the Lakeside Club was located upstairs over the store. Employees could recreate in the game room, play pool, or relax in the library. The club was also equipped with showers and toilets. (Courtesy of Marcia Evans.)

The Lake View House was home to many mill workers. Built in the late 1880s by the Merrick Thread Company, it was originally a smaller building before an addition made it markedly larger. In this photograph, Lake View House residents pose in front of the early, smaller boardinghouse. Notice there are only three gabled windows on the roof.

This photograph depicts the Lake View House after the addition was made, noticeable because of the appearance of two additional gabled windows on the roof. The building accommodated 120 regular boarders in addition to transient visitors. It was heated by steam and had electric lights and a shower and tub bath on each floor. The boardinghouse was furnished throughout and included complete laundry equipment and other modern conveniences.

Olympic Hall, the larger building on the left, was the town's public hall. It was there that suppers were served, concerts were performed by the Lake View Band, and basketball games were played. It even offered silent movies with live musical accompaniment.

This is another view of Olympic Hall. Private individuals owned it.

The second house from the upper-right corner was the Barchard house. The row of houses is opposite Olympic Hall. Notice the dirt road, the hill that leads up to Lake View's back street, and the electric poles. Electricity was furnished by the Lake View Electric Company, which operated two 40 kilowatt belted-unit generators. The company's service made it possible to light the mill, homes, and streetlights. (Courtesy of Marcia Evans.)

Lake View basketball players are seen in front of the post office about 1920. Lake View also had a tennis court and a baseball field in front of the Lake View House. For youngsters, a playground with swings, slides, and horizontal bars was located near the bandstand.

The Lake View Band, under the direction of Ralph Haskell, played at the village's bandstand. His sons played in the band, which sometimes boarded one of the mill's steamers to perform on Schoodic Lake.

Haskell's band, or the Lake View Band, was under the direction of Ralph Haskell. Occasionally they played outside the community. Pictured here, the band was one of four participants at Band Field Day at Camp Benson in Newport on August 26, 1923. Other bands performing were Fay and Scott from Dexter, Guilford Military Band, and the Pittsfield Band. (Courtesy of Isabelle Roberts.)

The Merrick Thread Company built the first school in Lake View in 1891. Later it was renovated and owned by the town. (Courtesy of Isabelle Roberts.)

Lake View's history includes several schools. Here is a photograph from the early 1900s of schoolchildren. Although all the names are not available, those identified, from left to right, are (first row) Linwood Hamlin, Helen Wright, Malcolm Heal, ? Barchard, unidentified, Robert Haskell, and Willis Hamlin; (second row) unidentified, Alan Wright, unidentified, unidentified, Evelyn Heal, unidentified, and Ella Barchard; (third row) Aubrey Haskell, Mildred Lewis, unidentified, Leo Heal, George Newman, and Gene Clark. (Courtesy of Isabelle Roberts.)

A new state-of-the-art school was built for Lake View children in 1919 to replace an old building that burned. The cost of construction was $20,000. The school accommodated about 100 pupils and taught all grades, including junior high and high school. Declining enrollment forced its closure after the American Thread Company went out of business. The few remaining children attended classes at the Lake View church.

After the new schoolhouse was closed, children attended classes in the Protestant church. One teacher taught all the children. By the time some reached the sixth grade, it was decided that even attendance there was too low. The children went to Milo for school. Isabelle Roberts remembers her mother driving her and several other youngsters to school in Milo. For eight weeks in the spring, the dirt roads were impassable, and the children had to remain at home.

Merrick Thread Company in Lake View joins in the festivities of what may be a Fourth of July parade. Notice Uncle Sam in the back row on the float.

Visit us at
arcadiapublishing.com

www.ingramcontent.com/pod-product-compliance
Lightning Source LLC
Chambersburg PA
CBHW050657110426
42813CB00007B/2039